VOL. 16

HAL•LEONARD®
KEYBOARD
PLAY-ALONG

1970s ROCK

ISBN 978-1-4234-6182-1

Visit Hal Leonard Online at **www.halleonard.com**

HAL•LEONARD®
CORPORATION
7777 W. BLUEMOUND RD. P.O. BOX 13819
MILWAUKEE, WISCONSIN 53213

VOL. 16

CONTENTS

Dream On

Words and Music by
Steven Tyler

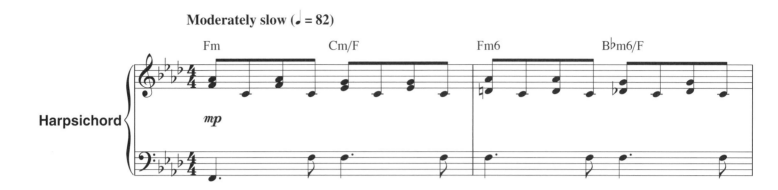

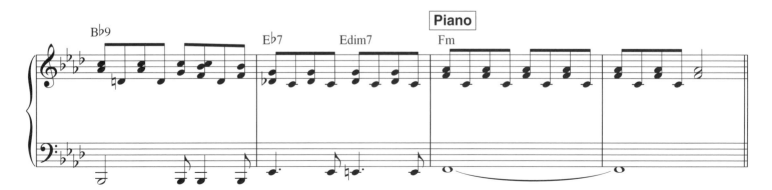

Ev -'ry time _____ that I look in the mir - ror,

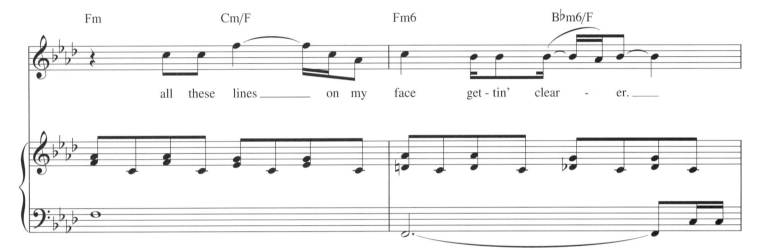

all these lines _____ on my face get - tin' clear - er. _____

The past ___ is gone. _____

It went by like _____ dusk to dawn. _____

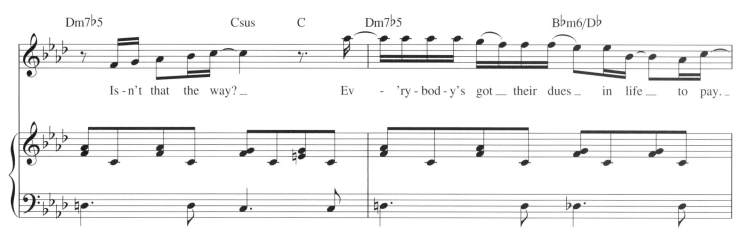

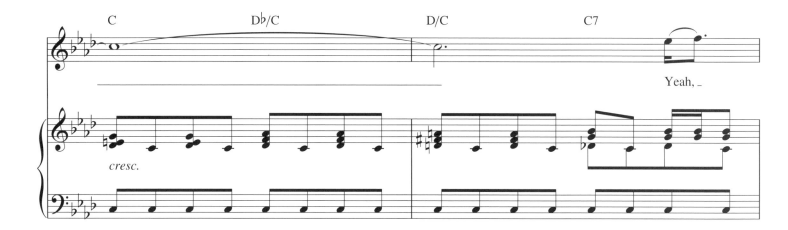

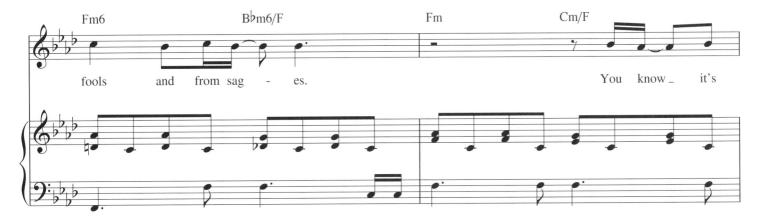

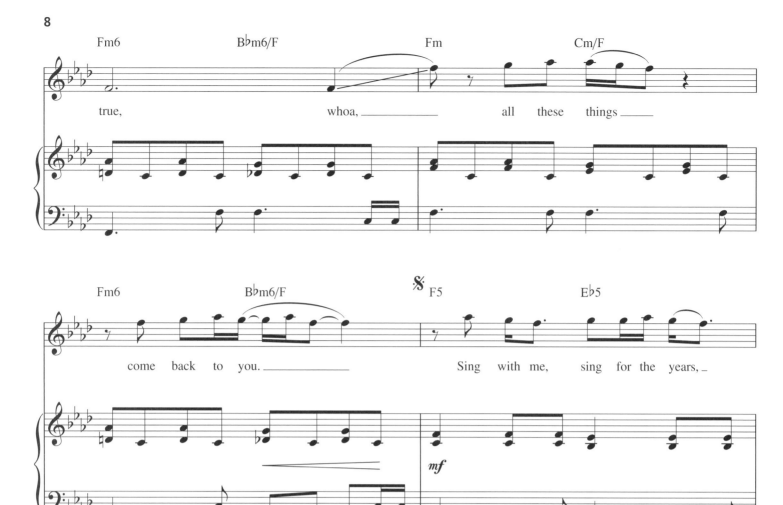

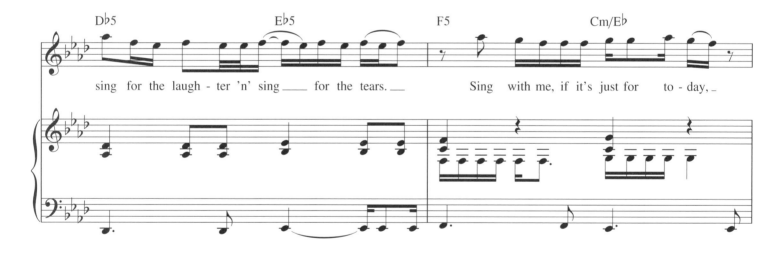

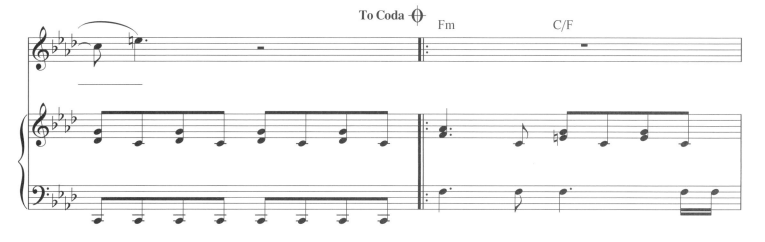

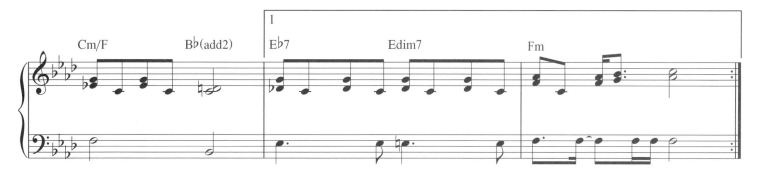

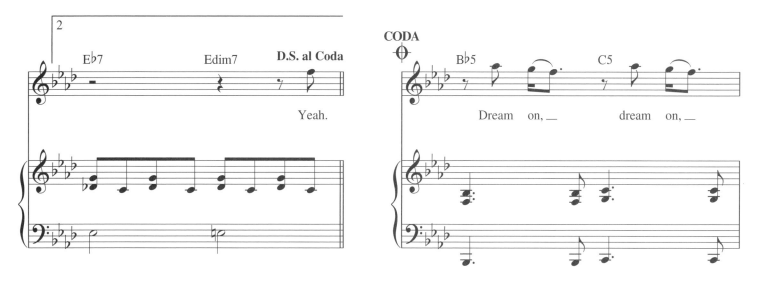

Dream on, — dream on, — dream on, — and dream un-til your dreams come —

— true.

Dream on, — dream on, — dream on, — dream on, — dream on, — dream on, —

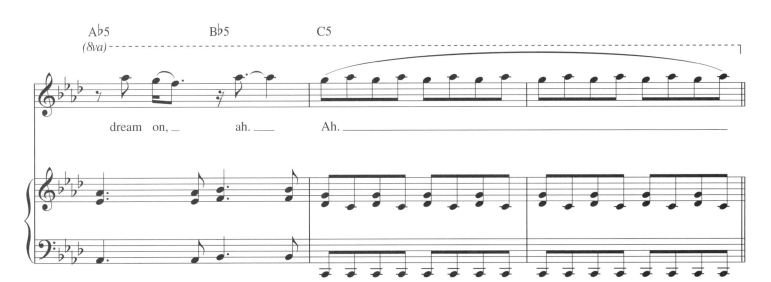

dream on, — ah. — Ah. —

Highway Star

Words and Music by Ritchie Blackmore, Ian Gillan,
Roger Glover, Jon Lord and Ian Paice

Fast driving Rock

Distorted Organ

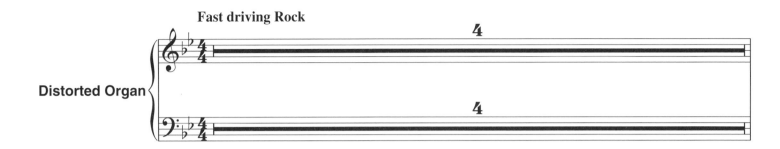

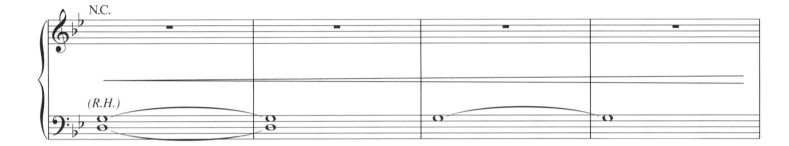

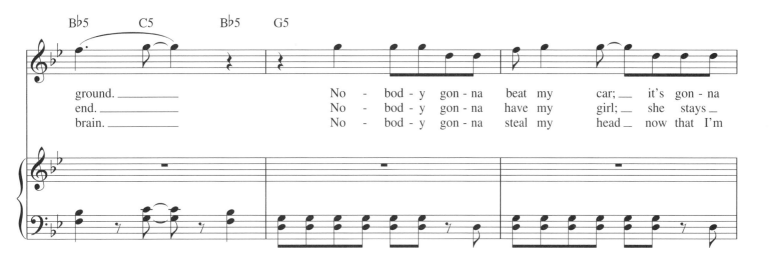

No - bod - y gon - na take my car; __ I'm gon - na race in - to the
No - bod - y gon - na take my girl; __ I'm gon - na keep her to the
No - bod - y gon - na take my head; __ I got __ speed in - side my

ground. _____
end. _____
brain. _____

No - bod - y gon - na beat my car; __ it's gon - na
No - bod - y gon - na have my girl; __ she stays __
No - bod - y gon - na steal my head __ now that I'm

break the speed of sound. _____ Ooh, it's a
close on ev - 'ry bend. _____ Ooh, she's a
on the road a - gain. _____ Ooh, I'm in

kill - ing ma - chine; _ it's got ev - 'ry - thing, ___
kill - ing ma - chine; _ she got ev - 'ry - thing, ___
heav - en a - gain; _ I got ev - 'ry - thing, ___

like a driv - ing pow'r, _ big fat tires _ and ev -
like a mov - ing mouth, _ bod - y con - trol _ and ev -
like a mov - ing ground, _ an o - pen road _ and ev -

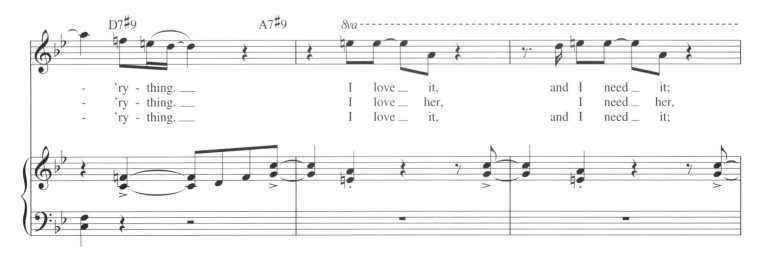

- 'ry - thing. ___ I love _ it, and I need _ it;
- 'ry - thing. ___ I love _ her, I need _ her,
- 'ry - thing. ___ I love _ it, and I need _ it;

I bleed _ it.
I seen _ her.
I seen _ it.

Yeah, _ it's a wild _
Yeah, _____ she turns _
Eight cyl - in - ders, all _____

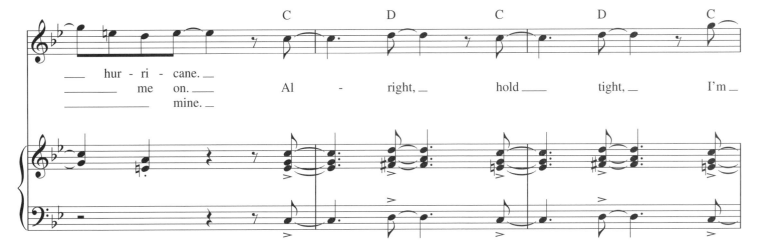

_ hur - ri - cane. _
_____ me on. _
_____ mine. _

Al - right, _ hold _____ tight, _ I'm _

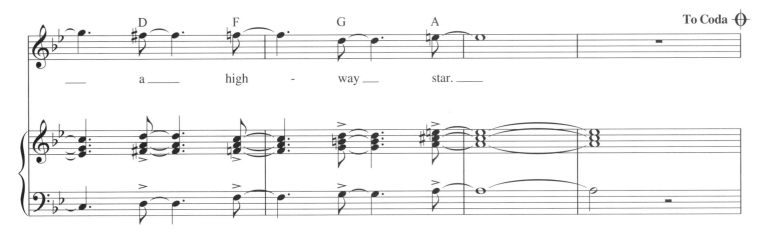

_ a _____ high - way _____ star. _____

To Coda ⊕

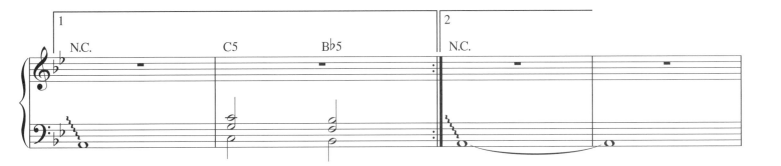

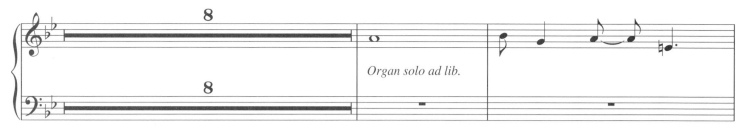

Organ solo ad lib.

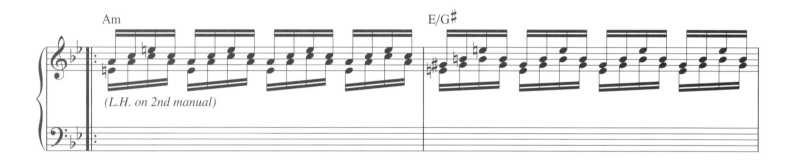

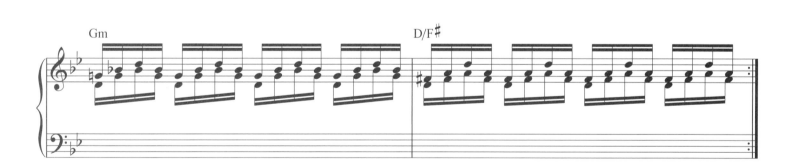

(L.H. on 2nd manual)

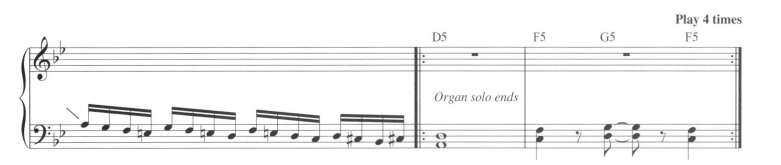

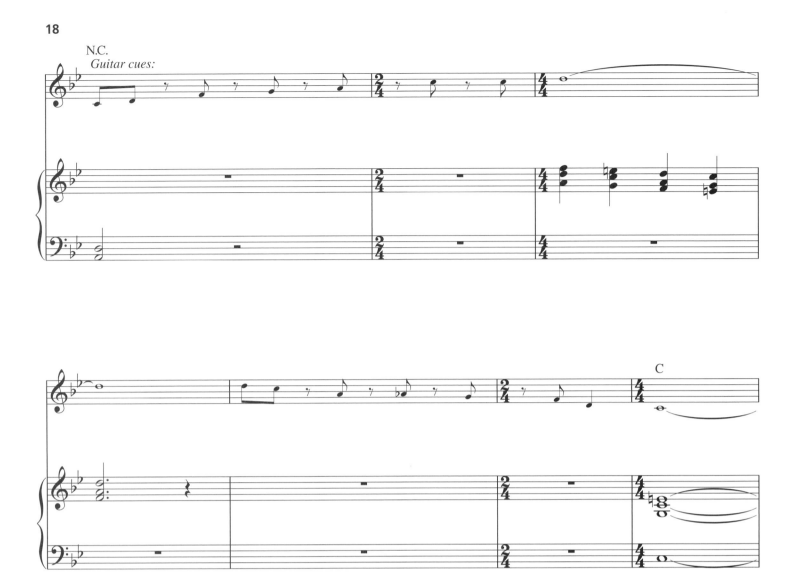

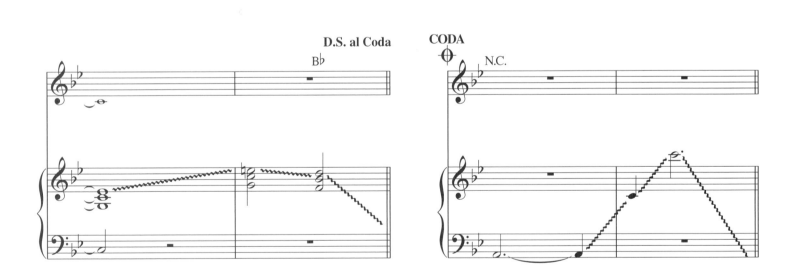

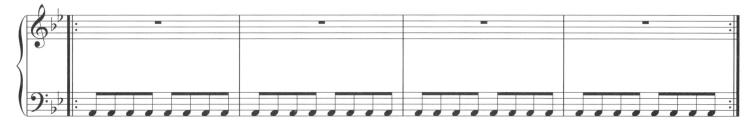

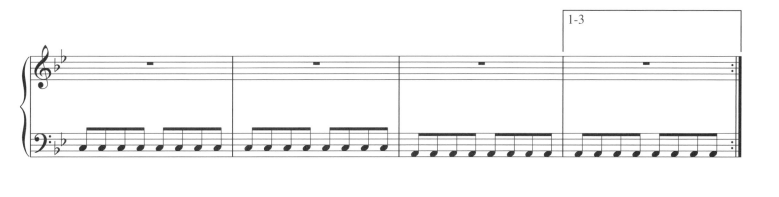

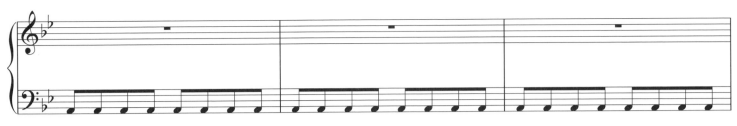

C5   Bb5   G5

Guitar solo ends   No - bod - y gon - na take my car; ___ I'm gon - na

(R.H.)

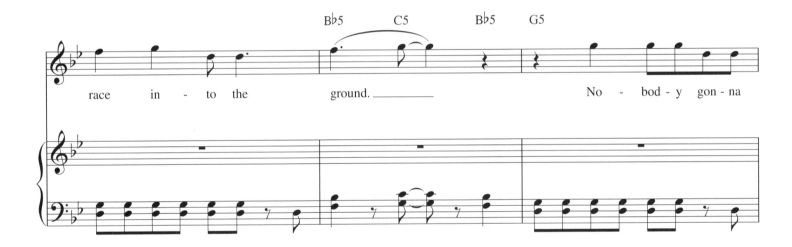

Bb5   C5   Bb5   G5

race in - to the   ground. ___   No - bod - y gon - na

Bb5   C5   Bb5

beat my car; ___ it's gon - na break the speed of   sound. ___

Ooh, it's a kill-ing ma-chine; ___ it's got ev - 'ry-thing, ___

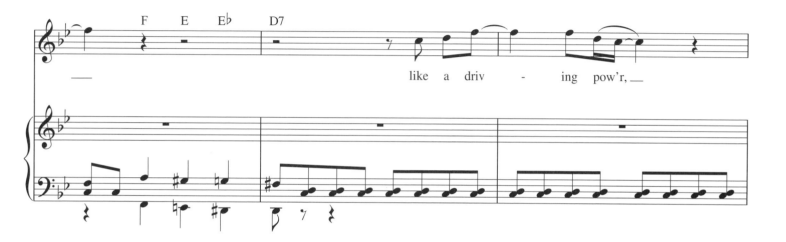

___ like a driv - ing pow'r, ___

big fat tires ___ and ev - 'ry-thing. ___ I love ___ it,

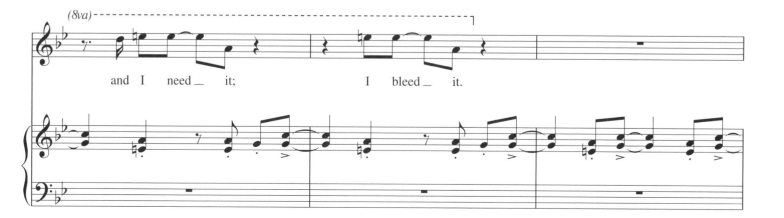

and I need ___ it; I bleed ___ it.

Yeah, _ it's a wild _ hur-ri-cane. _ Al - right, _ hold _

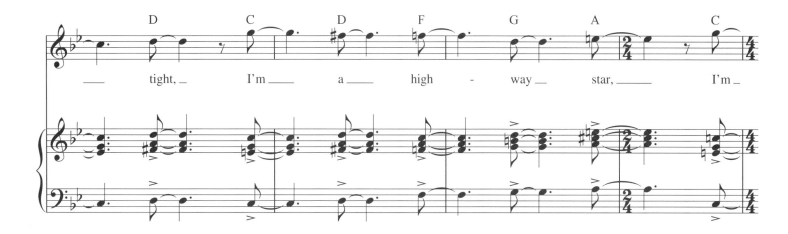

_ tight, _ I'm _ a _ high - way _ star, _ I'm _

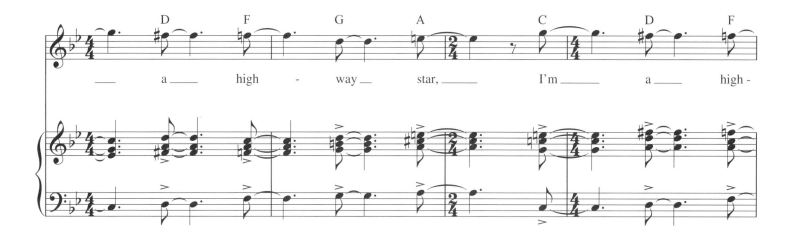

_ a _ high - way _ star, _ I'm _ a _ high -

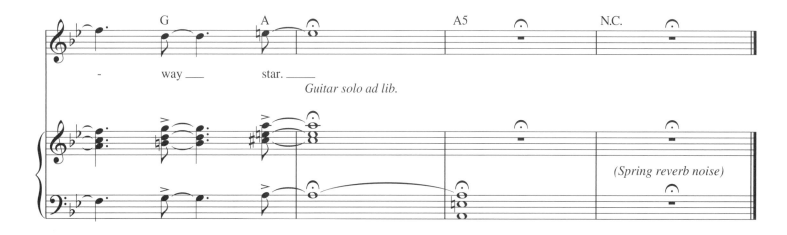

- way _ star. _

Guitar solo ad lib.

(Spring reverb noise)

I Feel the Earth Move

Words and Music by Carole King

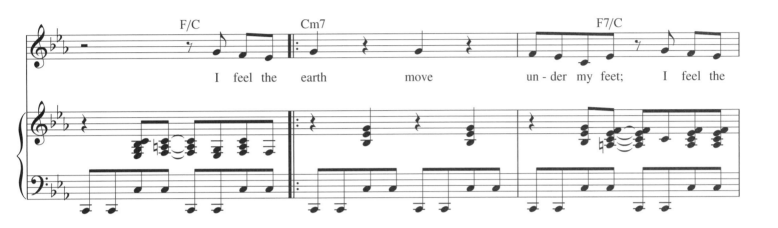

I feel the earth move un-der my feet; I feel the sky tum-bl-ing down. I feel my heart start to trem-bl-ing when-ev-er you're a-round. Ooh, ba-

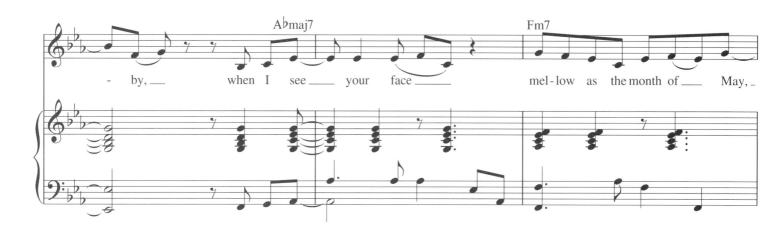

- by, __ when I see __ your face __ mel-low as the month of __ May, _

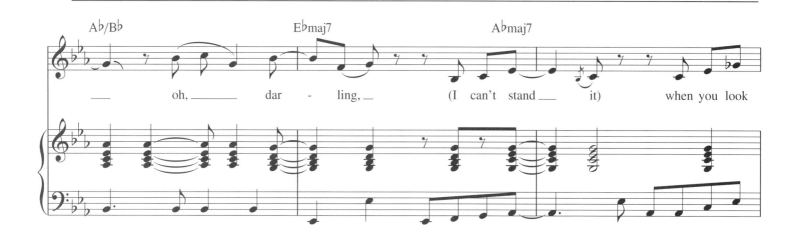

__ oh, __ dar - ling, __ (I can't stand __ it) when you look

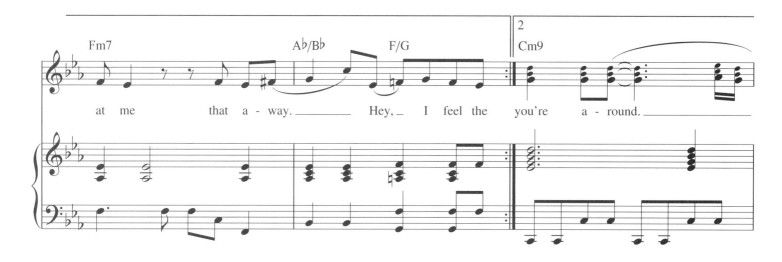

at me that a - way. __ Hey, _ I feel the you're a - round. __

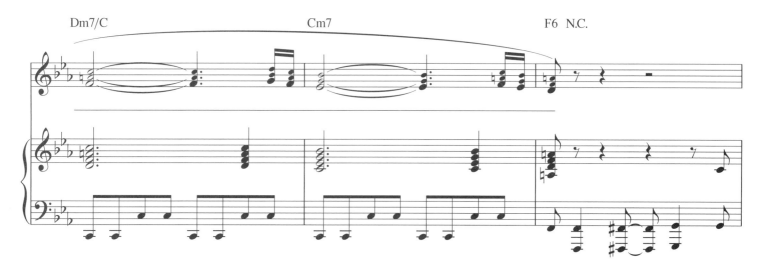

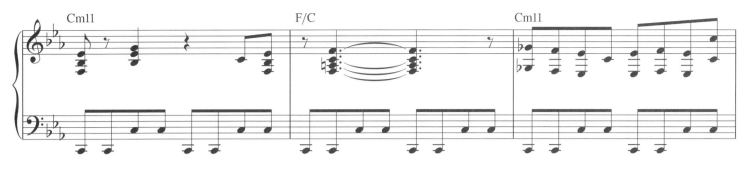

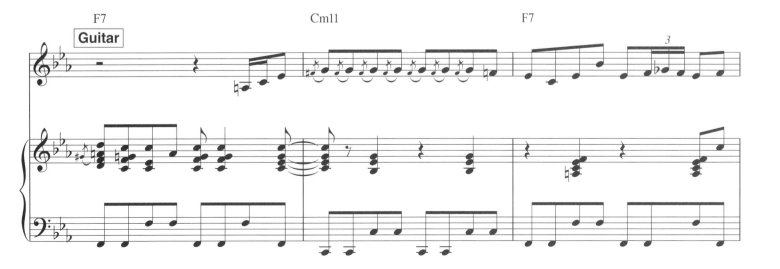

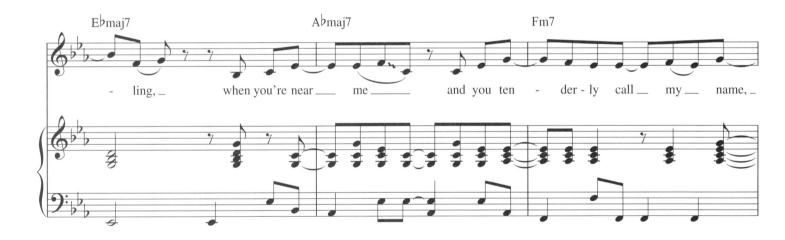

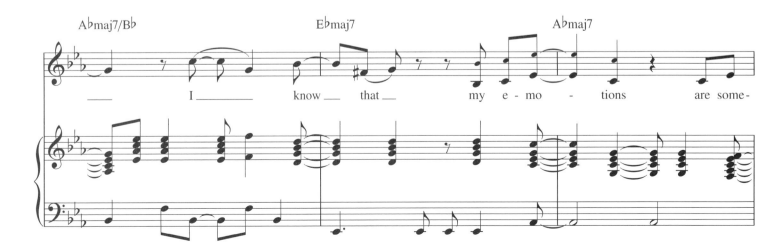

thing I just — can't tame. — I've just got to have — you, — ba - by. —

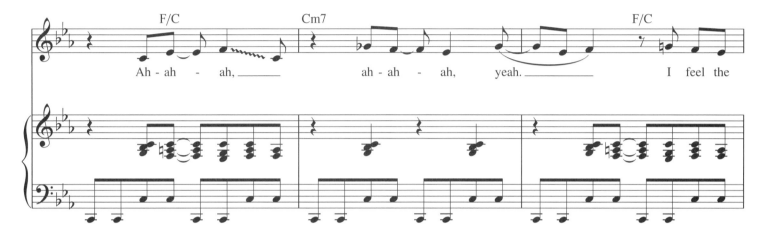

Ah - ah - ah, _____ ah - ah - ah, yeah. _____ I feel the

earth move un - der my feet; I feel the sky — tum - bl - ing down, a -

tum - bl - ing down. I feel the earth move _____ un - der my feet. I feel the

sky __ tum- bl- ing down, a- tum- bl- ing down. __ I just a- lose con- trol __

__ down to my ver - y soul. _____ I get a-

hot and cold _____ all o - ver, all o - ver, all o-

- ver, all o - ver. I feel the earth move un- der my feet; I feel the

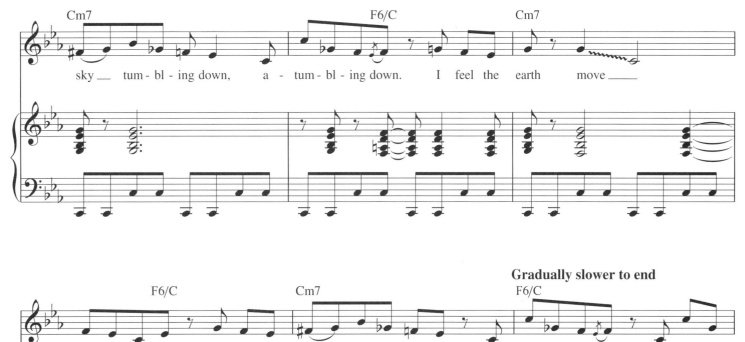

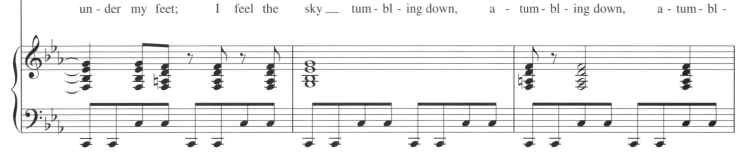

Gradually slower to end

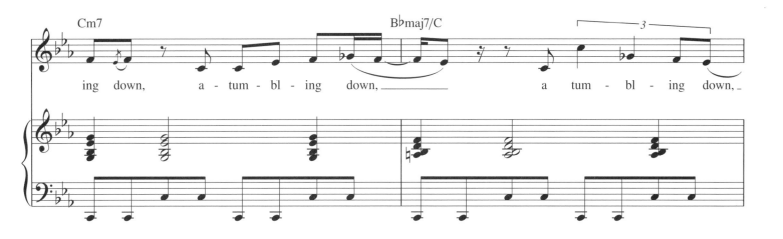

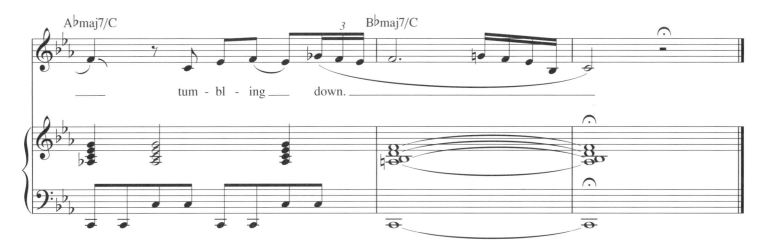

Foreplay/Long Time
(Long Time)

Words and Music by
Tom Scholz

Very fast Rock

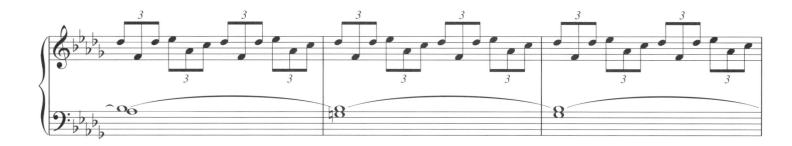

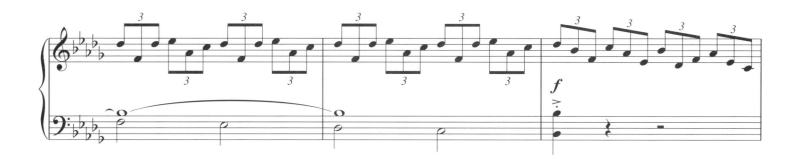

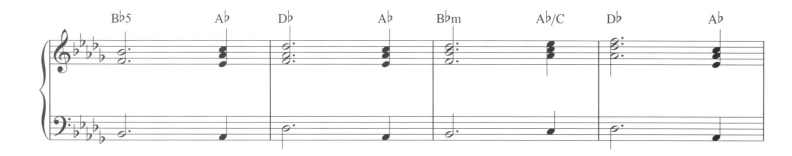

Slowly and freely

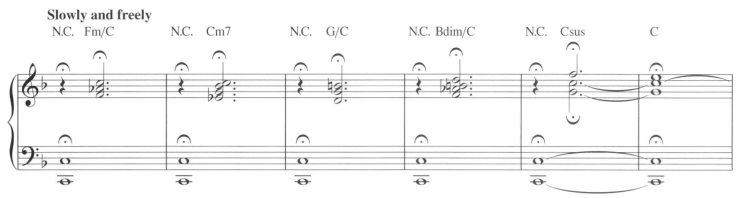

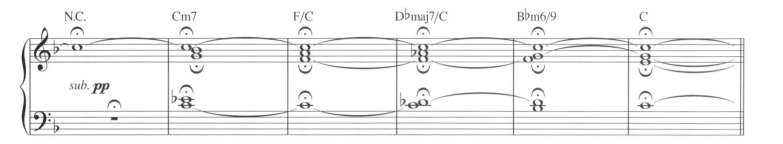

Moderate Rock

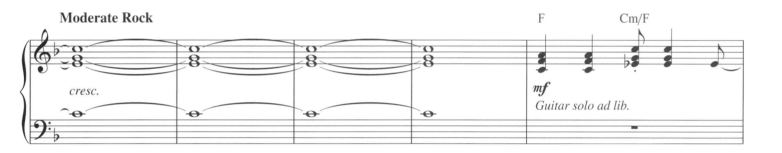

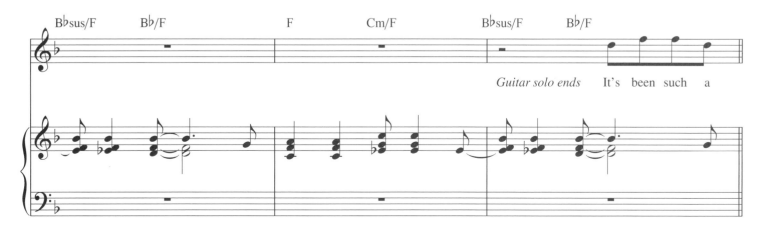

Guitar solo ends It's been such a

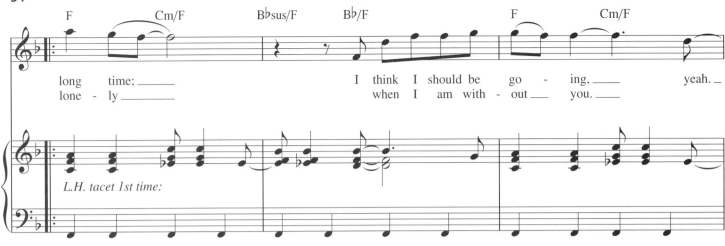

long time; _____
lone - ly _____

I think I should be go - ing, _____ yeah. _____
when I am with - out _____ you. _____

L.H. tacet 1st time:

_____ And time does - n't wait for me; _____ it keeps on roll -
But in my mind, _____ deep in my mind, _____ I can't for - get a -

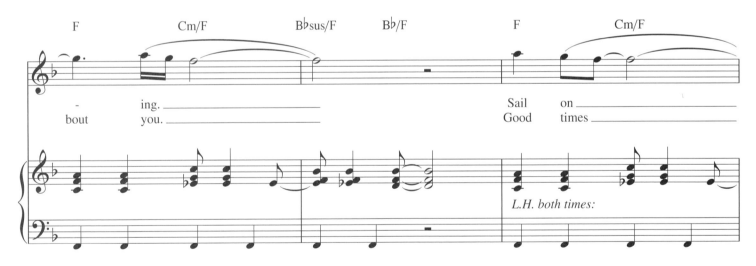

- ing. _____
bout you. _____

Sail on _____
Good times _____

L.H. both times:

_____ on a dis - tant high - way, _____ yeah. _____ I've got to
_____ and fac - es that re - mind _ me, _____ yeah. _____ I'm

keep on ___ chas-ing a dream; ___ I've got-ta be on my ___ way. ___
try'n' to for-get your ___ name ___ and leave it all be-hind ___ me; ___

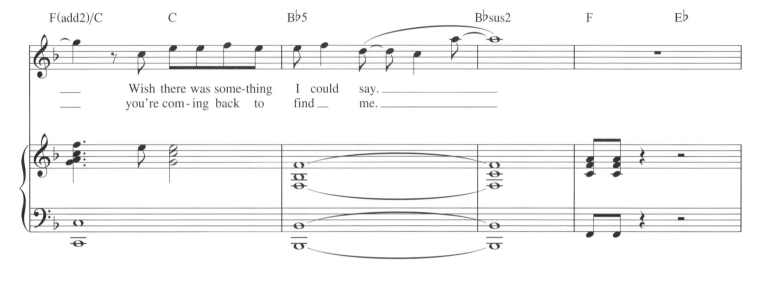

___ Wish there was some-thing I could say. ___
___ you're com-ing back to find ___ me. ___

Well, I'm tak-ing my time, __ I'm just __ mov-ing a-long. __

You'll for-get a-bout __ me af-ter I've been gone. __ And I take what I find; __ I don't __

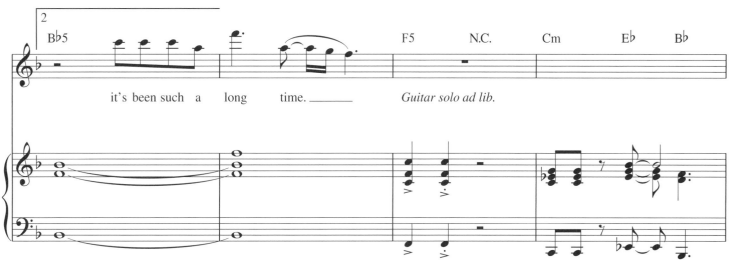

it's been such a long time. _____ *Guitar solo ad lib.*

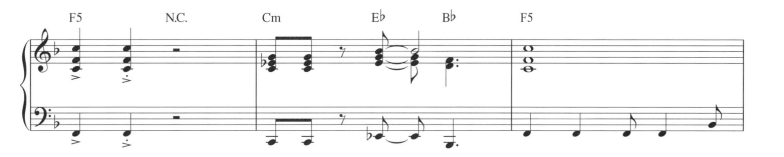

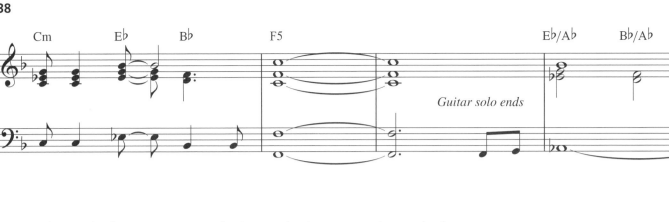

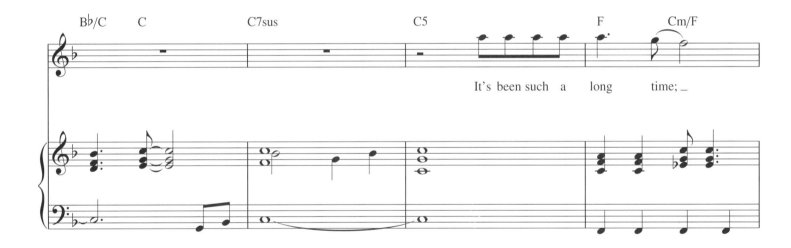

time does-n't wait for me; _____ it keeps on roll - ing. _____

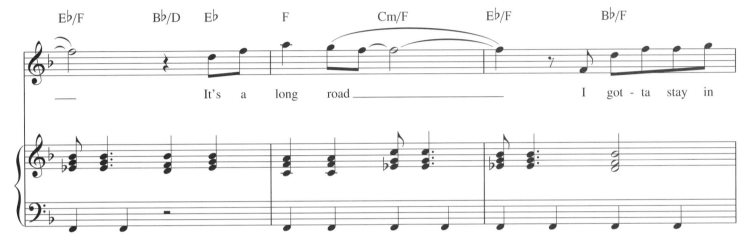

____ It's a long road _____ I got-ta stay in

time with, ____ yeah. _____ I've got to keep on ____ chas-ing that dream, _

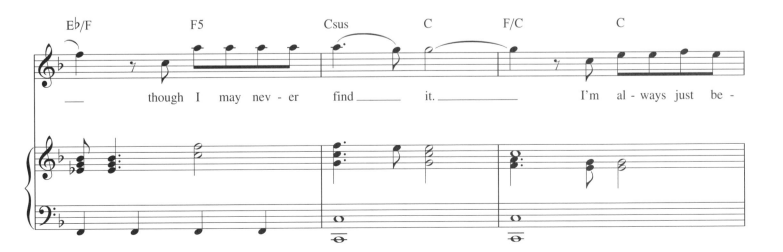

____ though I may nev - er find _____ it. _____ I'm al - ways just be -

Sweet Home Alabama

Words and Music by Ronnie Van Zant,
Ed King and Gary Rossington

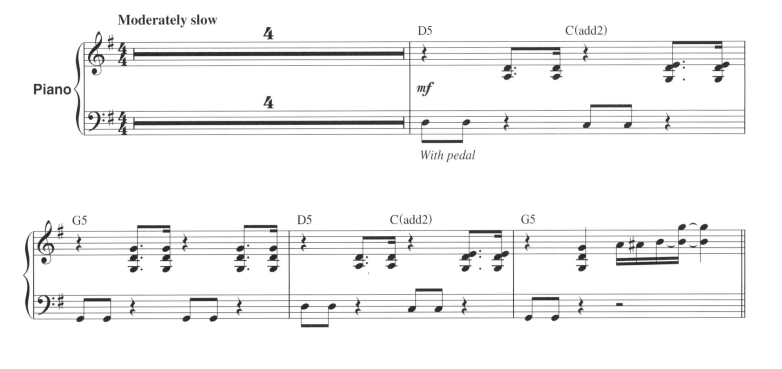

Big ___ wheels, ___ keep on turn - in';
Well, I heard Mis - ter Young ___ sing a - bout ___ her;

car - ry me home to my kin. ___
Well, I heard ol' Neil put her down. ___

Sing - in' songs a - bout __ the South - land;
Well, I hope Neil Young __ will __ re - mem - ber:

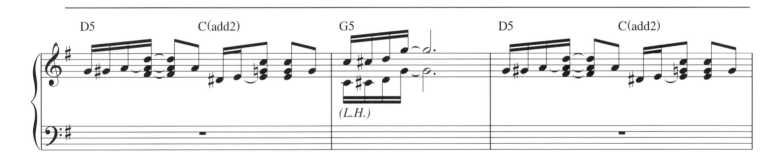

I miss Al - a - bam - y once a - gain, __ and I think it's a sin, __ yes.
a South - ern __ man __ don't need him a -

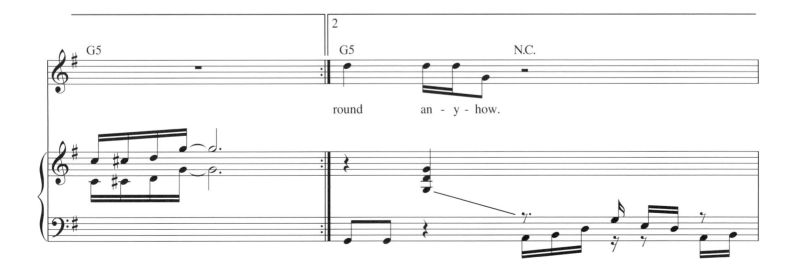

round an - y - how.

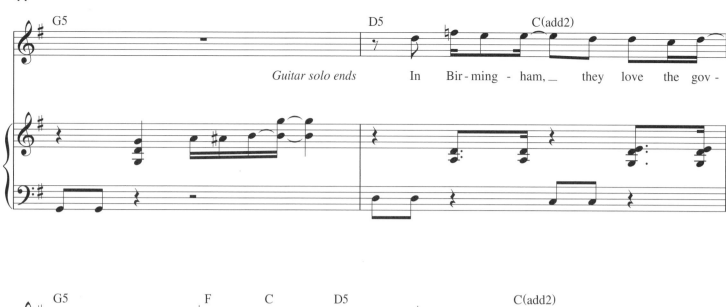

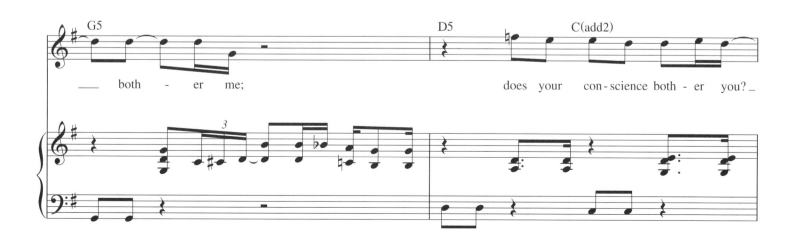

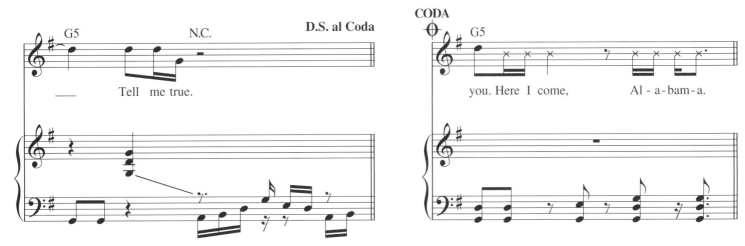

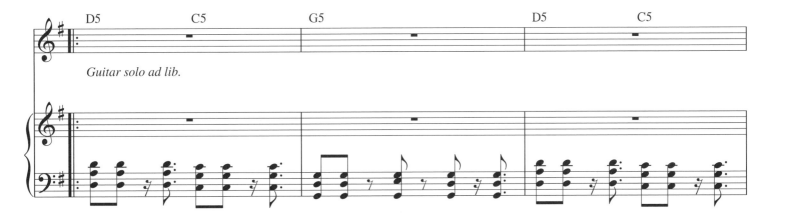

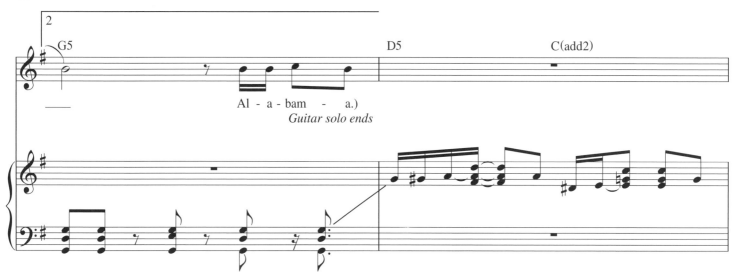

Al - a - bam - a.)
Guitar solo ends

Now, Mus-cle Shoals_ has got the Swamp - ers;

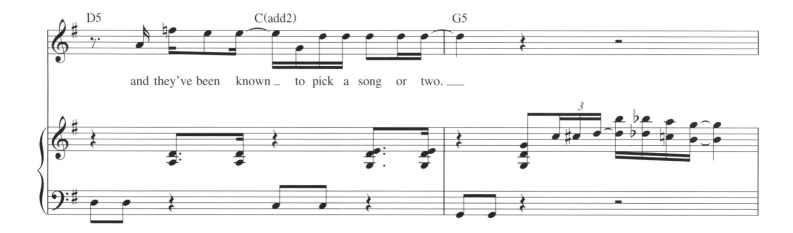

and they've been known_ to pick a song or two.___

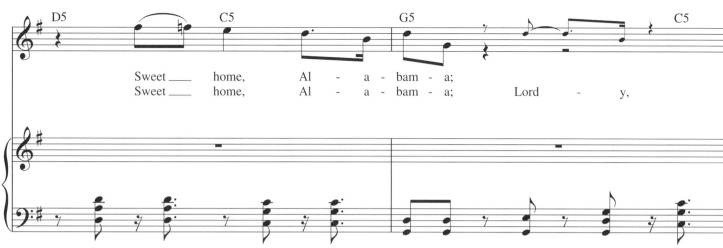

Sweet _____ home, Al - a - bam - a;
Sweet _____ home, Al - a - bam - a; Lord - y,

Lord, _ I'm com - in' home to you. you.

Piano solo ad lib.

Point of Know Return

Words and Music by Steve Walsh,
Phil Ehart and Robert Steinhardt

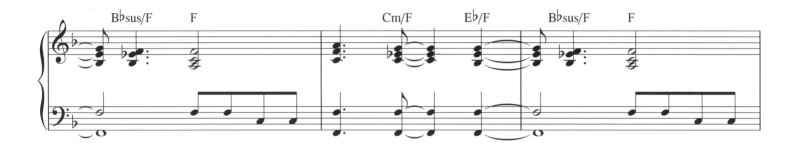

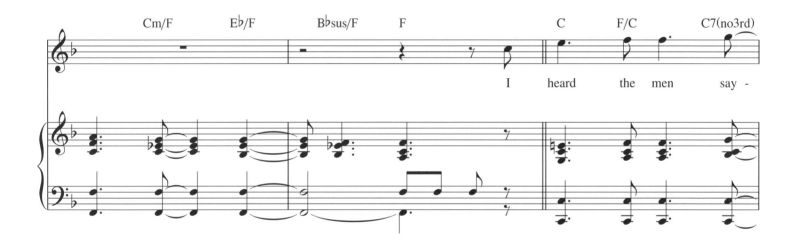

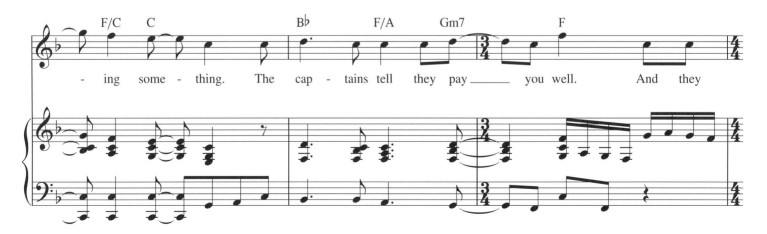

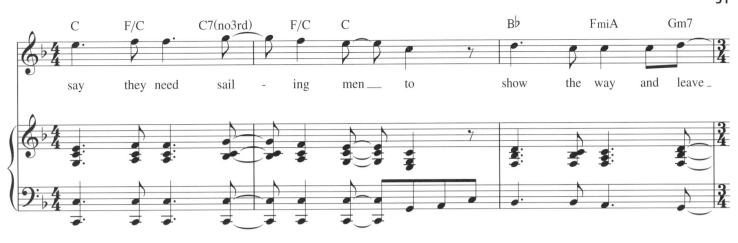

say they need sail - ing men __ to show the way and leave __

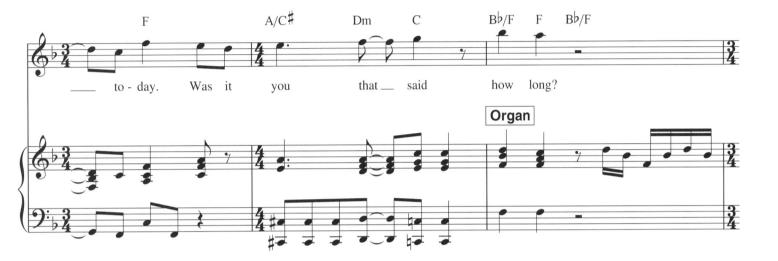

__ to - day. Was it you that __ said how long?

Organ

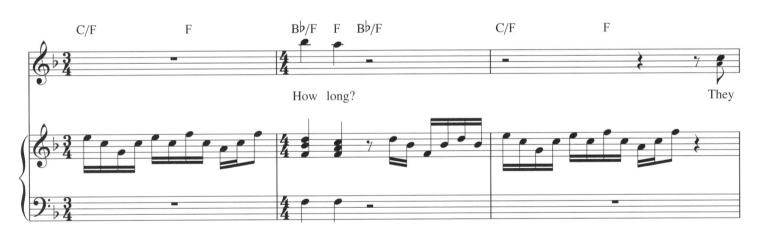

How long? They

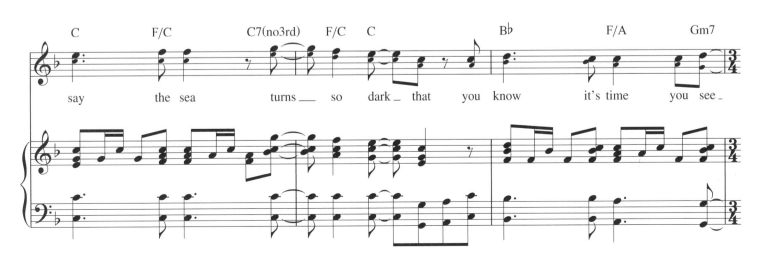

say the sea turns __ so dark __ that you know it's time you see __

the sign. They say the point de - mons guard __ is an

o - cean grave for all _____ the brave. Was it you that __ said

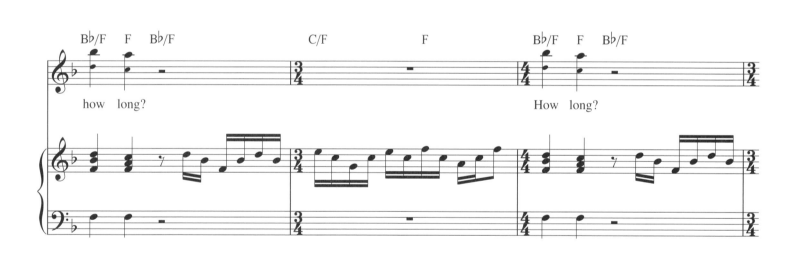

how long? How long?

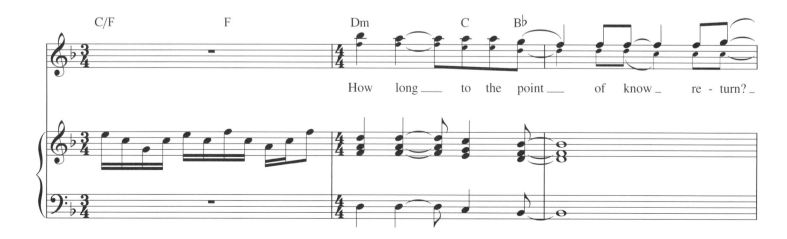

How long ____ to the point ____ of know _ re - turn? _

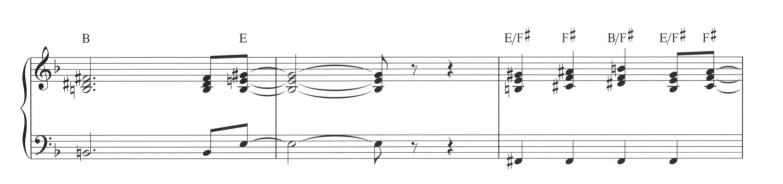

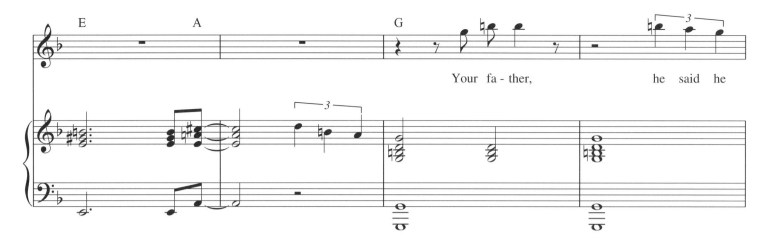

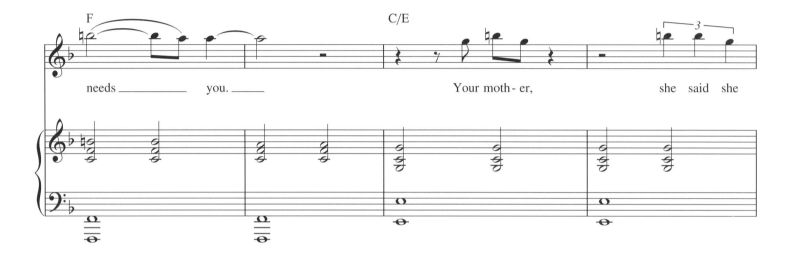

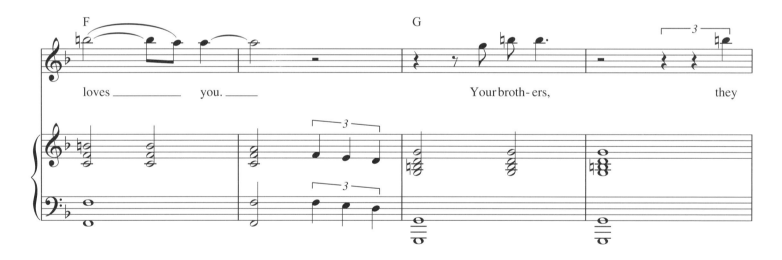

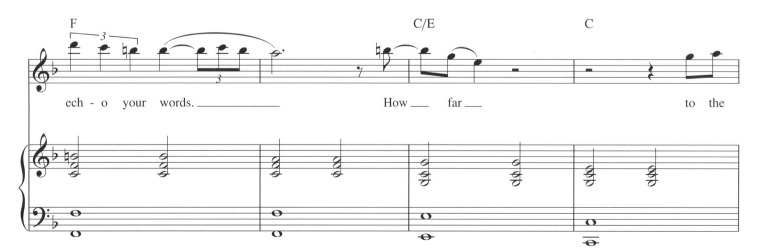

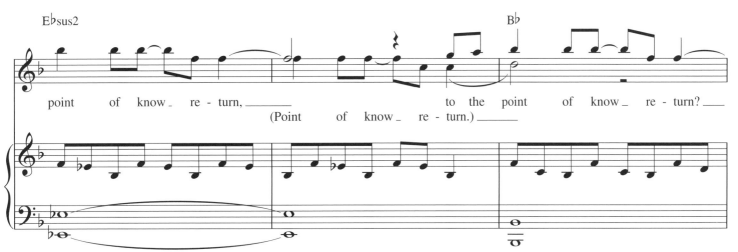

point of know _ re - turn, _____ to the point of know _ re - turn? ____

(Point of know _ re - turn.) _____

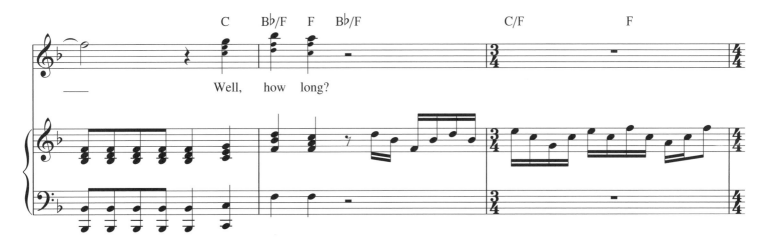

_____ Well, how long?

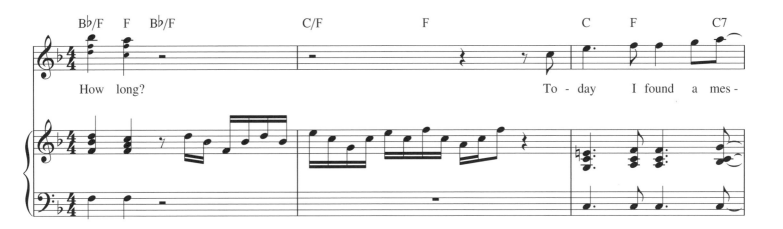

How long? To - day I found a mes -

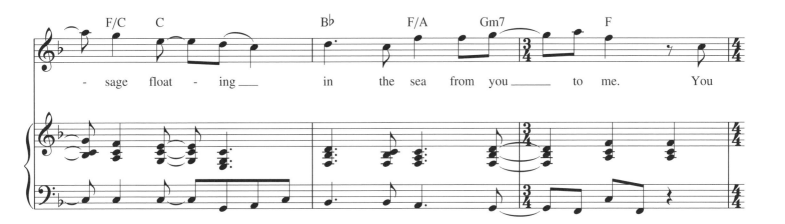

- sage float - ing ___ in the sea from you ___ to me. _____ You

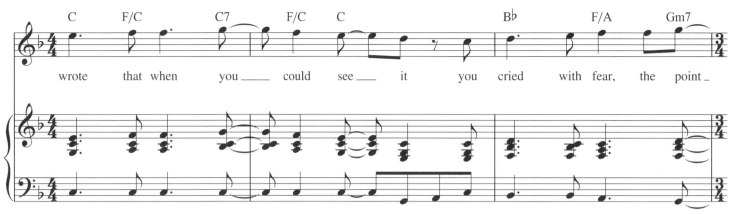

wrote that when you ____ could see ____ it you cried with fear, the point ____

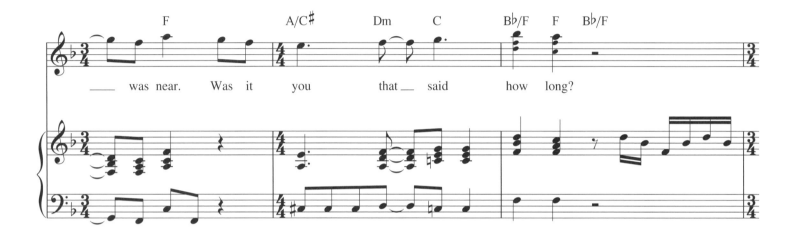

____ was near. Was it you that ____ said how long?

How long?

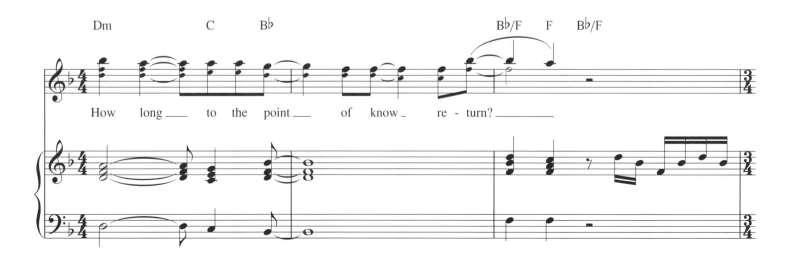

How long ____ to the point ____ of know ____ re - turn? _____

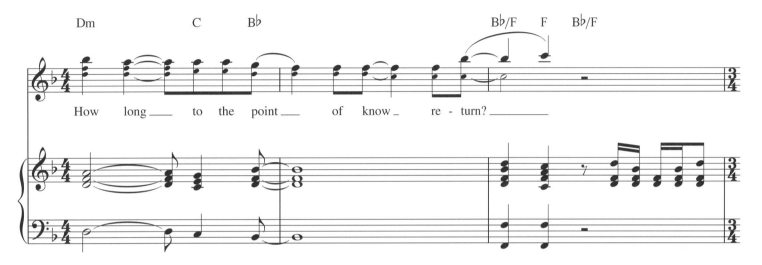

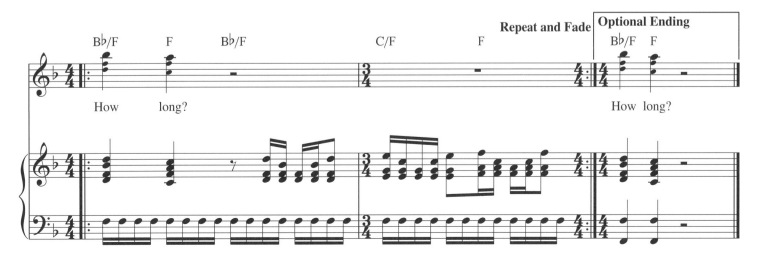

Take the Long Way Home

Words and Music by Rick Davies
and Roger Hodgson

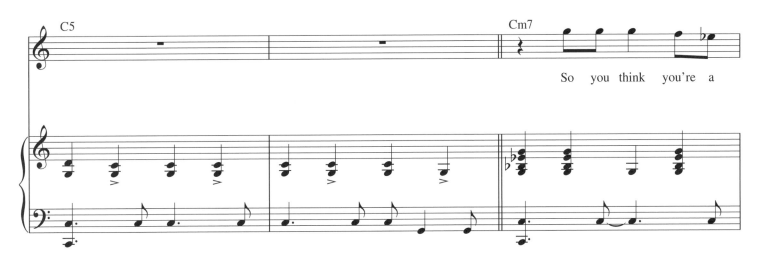

So you think you're a

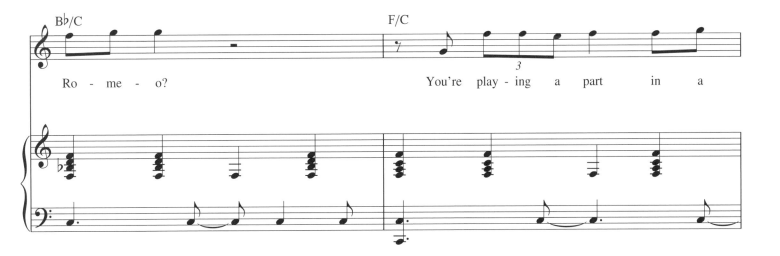

Ro - me - o? You're play-ing a part in a

pic - ture show. Well, take the long way home, take the

long way home. If you're the joke of the

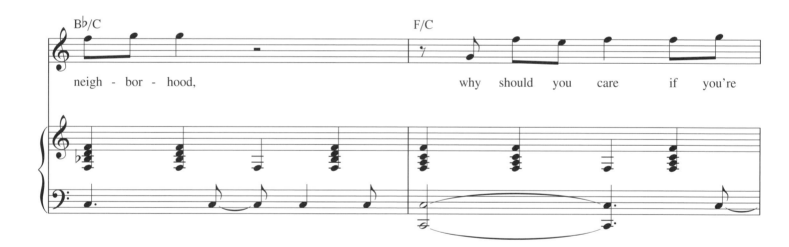

neigh - bor - hood, why should you care if you're

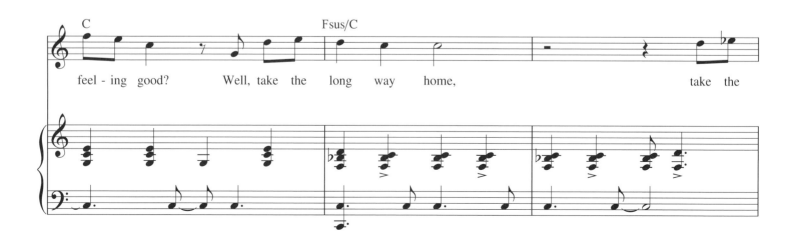

feel - ing good? Well, take the long way home, take the

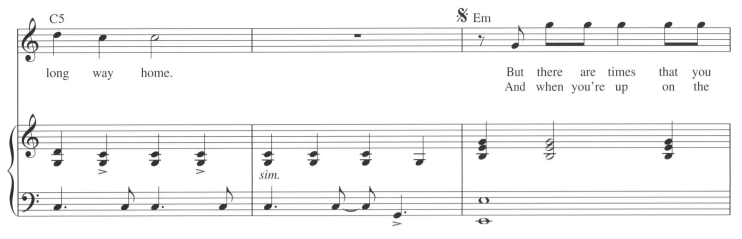

long way home.
But there are times that you
And when you're up on the

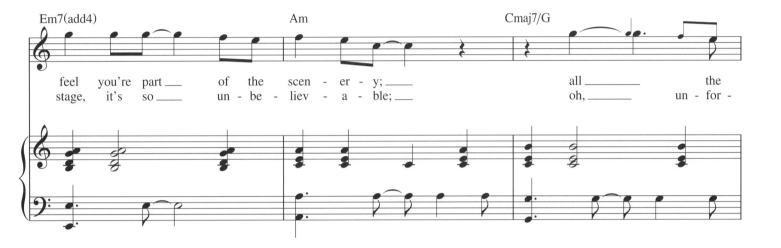

feel you're part ___ of the scen - er - y; ___ all ___ the
stage, it's so ___ un - be - liev - a - ble; ___ oh, ___ un - for -

green - er - y ___ is com - ing down, ___
get - ta - ble ___ how they a - dore ___

boy.
And then your wife seems to think you're part ___ of the
you.
But then your wife seems to think you're los - ing your

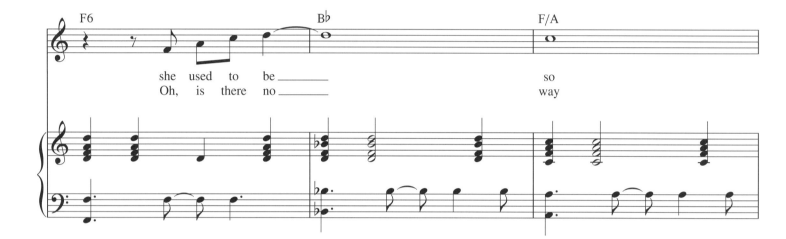

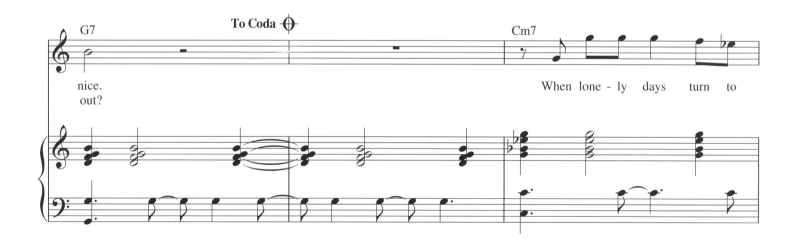

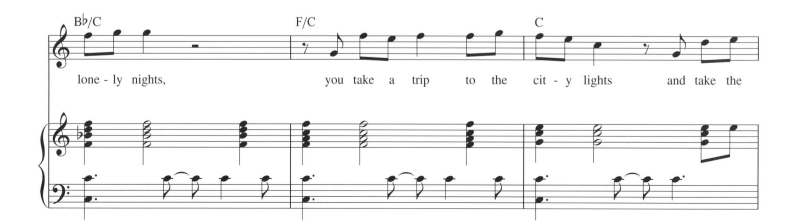

long way home, take the long way home.

You nev-er see what you wan-na see;

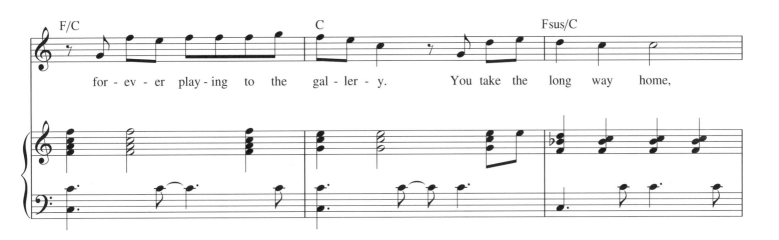

for-ev-er play-ing to the gal-ler-y. You take the long way home,

D.S. al Coda

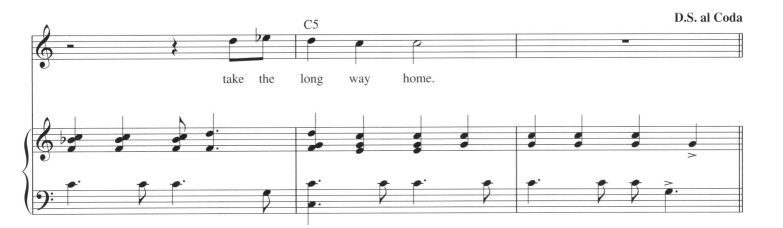

take the long way home.

CODA

Oh, yeah. *Solos ad lib.*

Oh, do you feel that your life's be - come __ a ca - tas - tro - phe? __

Oh, _____ it has to be _____ for you to grow, _

_ boy. Oh, when you look through the

years and see ___ what you could have been, _ oh, what you

might have been, _ if you had had _____

Do it a-gain, __ took the Took the long way home.

Took the long way home.

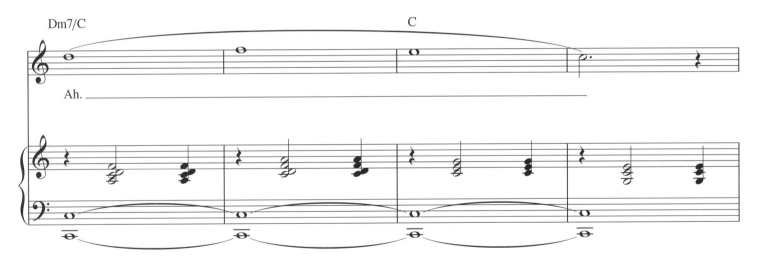

Ah. __

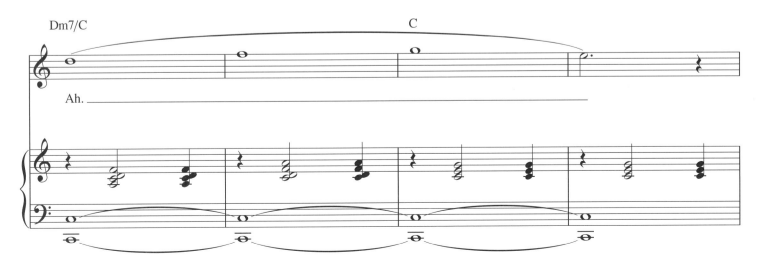

Ah. __

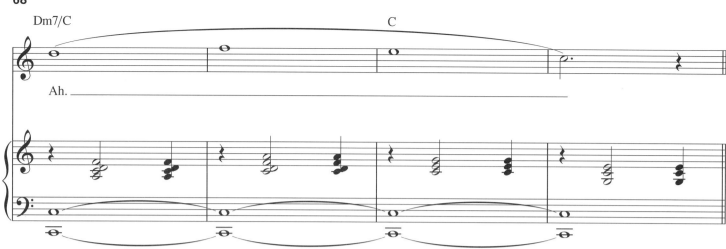

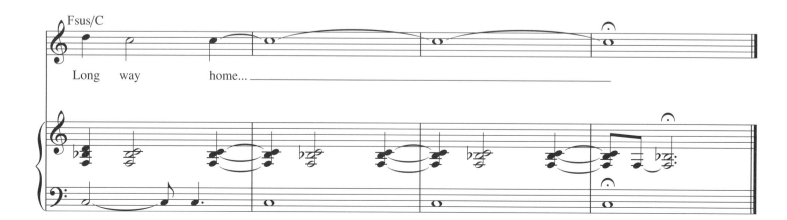

Will It Go Round in Circles

Words and Music by Billy Preston
and Bruce Fisher

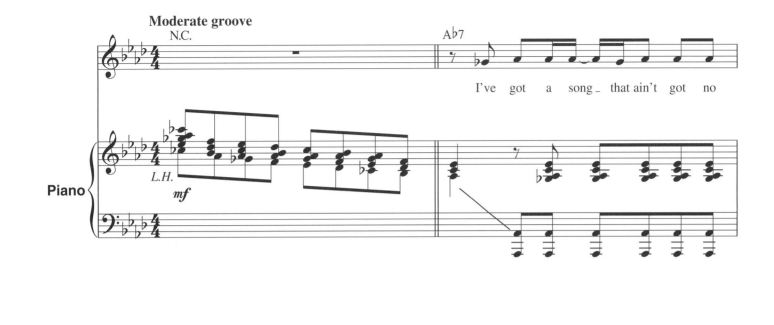

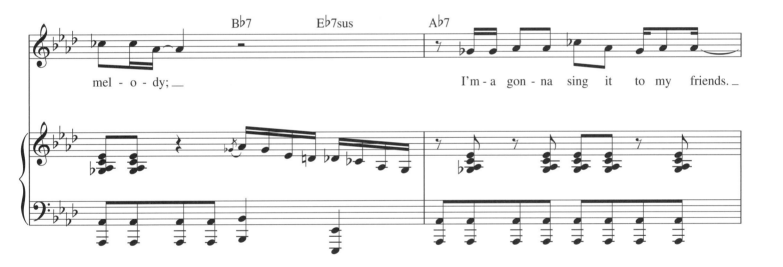

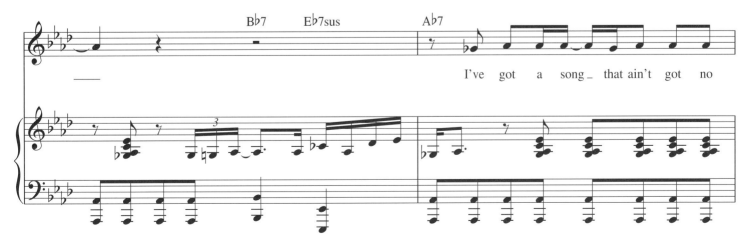

Will it fly high like a bird up in the sky? _____

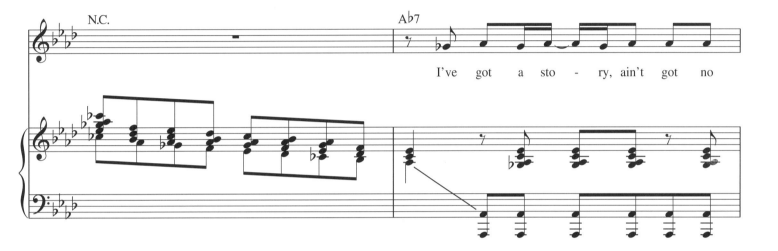

I've got a sto - ry, ain't got no

mor - al; _____ let the bad guy win ev - 'ry once in a while. _

_ I've got a sto - ry, ain't got no

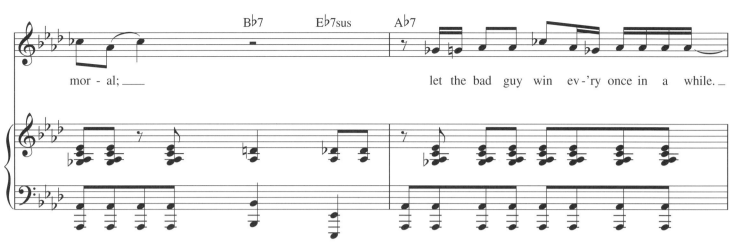

mor - al; ___   let the bad guy win ev-'ry once in a while. ___

___   Will it go 'round in cir - cles?

Will it fly high like a bird up in the sky? _____

Will it go 'round in cir - cles?

Will it fly high like a bird up in the sky? ____

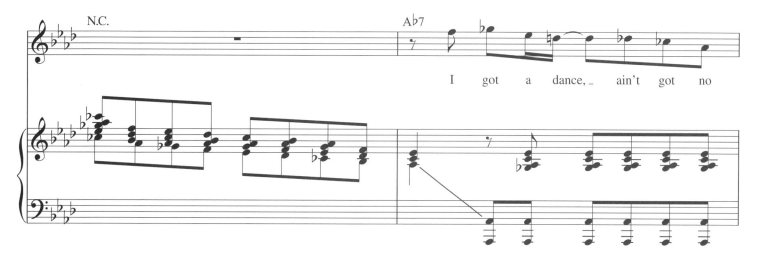

I got a dance, _ ain't got no

steps, no; I'm gon-na let the mu-sic move me a-

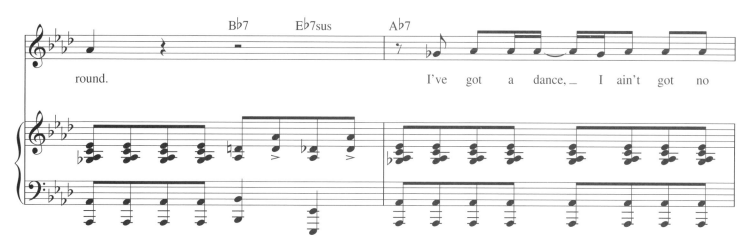

round. I've got a dance, _ I ain't got no

steps; I'm gon-na let the mu-sic move me a-

round. _____ Will it go 'round in cir - cles?

Will it fly high like a bird up in the sky? _

Will it go 'round in cir - cles?

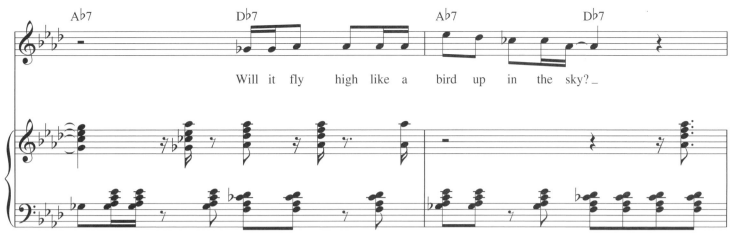

Will it fly high like a bird up in the sky? _

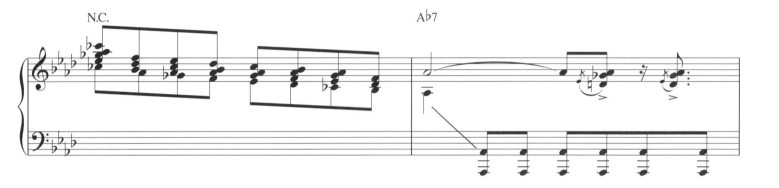

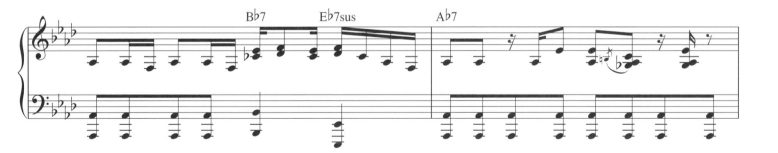

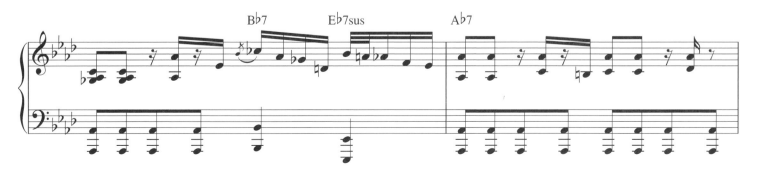

Will it go 'round in cir - cles? _____

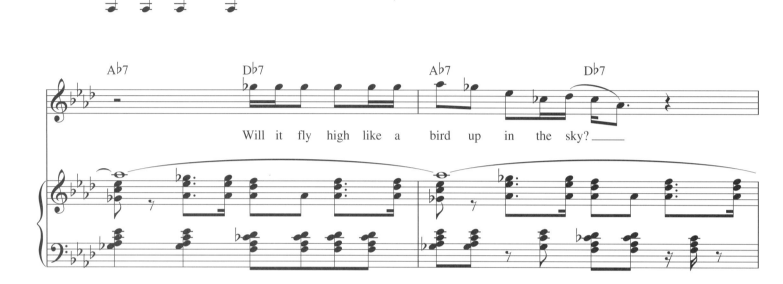

Will it fly high like a bird up in the sky? _____

Will it go 'round in cir - cles? _____

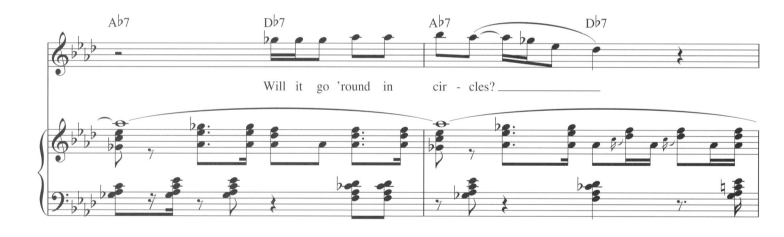

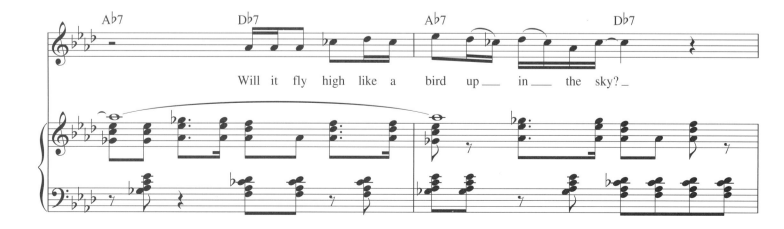

Will it fly high like a bird up ___ in ___ the sky? __

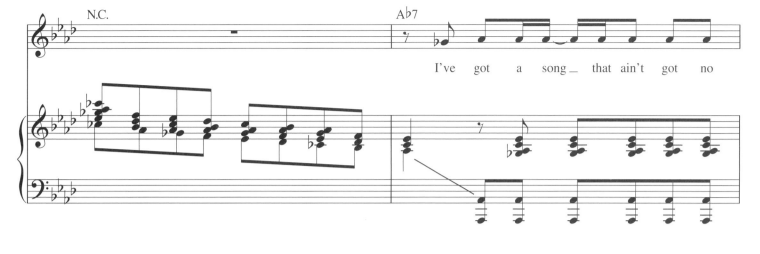

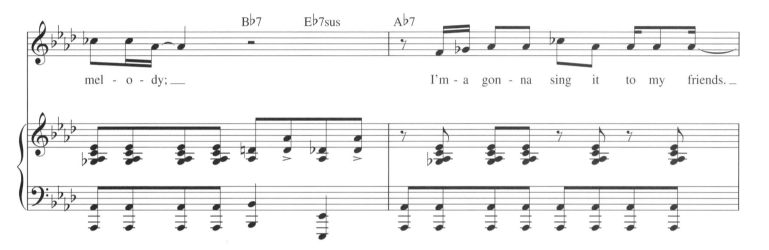

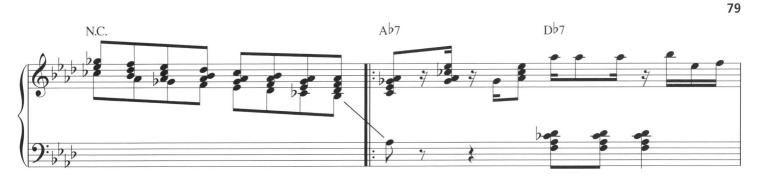

HAL·LEONARD
KEYBOARD
PLAY-ALONG

The **Keyboard Play-Along** series will help you quickly and easily play your favorite songs as played by your favorite artists. Just follow the music in the book, listen to the CD to hear how the keyboard should sound, and then play along using the separate backing tracks. The melody and lyrics are also included in the book in case you want to sing, or simply to help you follow along. The audio CD is playable on any CD player. For PC and Mac users, the CD is enhanced so you can adjust the recording to any tempo without changing pitch! Each book/CD pack in this series features eight great songs.

1. POP/ROCK HITS
Against All Odds (Take a Look at Me Now) • Deacon Blues • (Everything I Do) I Do It for You • Hard to Say I'm Sorry • Kiss on My List • My Life • Walking in Memphis • What a Fool Believes.
00699875 Keyboard Transcriptions $14.95

2. SOFT ROCK
Don't Know Much • Glory of Love • I Write the Songs • It's Too Late • Just Once • Making Love Out of Nothing at All • We've Only Just Begun • You Are the Sunshine of My Life.
00699876 Keyboard Transcriptions $12.95

3. CLASSIC ROCK
Against the Wind • Come Sail Away • Don't Do Me like That • Jessica • Say You Love Me • Takin' Care of Business • Werewolves of London • You're My Best Friend.
00699877 Keyboard Transcriptions $14.95

4. CONTEMPORARY ROCK
Angel • Beautiful • Because of You • Don't Know Why • Fallin' • Listen to Your Heart • A Thousand Miles • Unfaithful.
00699878 Keyboard Transcriptions $14.95

5. ROCK HITS
Back at One • Brick • Clocks • Drops of Jupiter (Tell Me) • Home • 100 Years • This Love • You're Beautiful
00699879 Keyboard Transcriptions $14.95

6. ROCK BALLADS
Bridge over Troubled Water • Easy • Hey Jude • Imagine • Maybe I'm Amazed • A Whiter Shade of Pale • You Are So Beautiful • Your Song.
00699880 Keyboard Transcriptions $14.95

7. ROCK CLASSICS
Baba O'Riley • Bloody Well Right • Carry on Wayward Son • Changes • Cold As Ice • Evil Woman • Space Truckin' • That's All.
00699881 Keyboard Transcriptions $14.95

8. BILLY JOEL – CLASSICS
Angry Young Man • Captain Jack • Honesty • Movin' Out (Anthony's Song) • My Life • Only the Good Die Young • Piano Man • Summer, Highland Falls.
00700302 Keyboard Transcriptions $14.99

9. ELTON JOHN BALLADS
Blue Eyes • Candle in the Wind • Daniel • Don't Let the Sun Go Down on Me • Goodbye Yellow Brick Road • Rocket Man (I Think It's Gonna Be a Long Long Time) • Someone Saved My Life Tonight • Sorry Seems to Be the Hardest Word.
00700752 Keyboard Transcriptions $14.99

10. STEELY DAN
Aja • Do It Again • FM • Hey Nineteen • Peg • Reeling in the Years • Rikki Don't Lose That Number.
00700201 Keyboard Transcriptions $14.99

11. THE DOORS
Break on Through to the Other Side • Hello, I Love You (Won't You Tell Me Your Name?) • L.A. Woman • Light My Fire • Love Me Two Times • People Are Strange • Riders on the Storm • Roadhouse Blues.
00699886 Keyboard Transcriptions $14.95

12. CHRISTMAS HITS
Baby, It's Cold Outside • Blue Christmas • Merry Christmas, Darling • Mistletoe and Wine • Santa Baby • A Spaceman Came Travelling • Step into Christmas • Wonderful Christmastime.
00700267 Keyboard Transcriptions $14.95

13. BILLY JOEL – HITS
Allentown • Just the Way You Are • New York State of Mind • Pressure • Root Beer Rag • Scenes from an Italian Restaurant • She's Always a Woman • Tell Her About It.
00700303 Keyboard Transcriptions $14.99

14. LENNON & McCARTNEY
All You Need Is Love • Back in the U.S.S.R. • Come Together • Get Back • Good Day Sunshine • Hey Jude • Penny Lane • Revolution.
00700754 Keyboard Transcriptions $14.99

15. ELVIS PRESLEY
All Shook Up • A Big Hunk O' Love • Blue Suede Shoes • Can't Help Falling in Love • Don't Be Cruel (To a Heart That's True) • I Want You, I Need You, I Love You • Jailhouse Rock • Love Me.
00700755 Keyboard Transcriptions $14.99

16. 1970s ROCK
Dream On • Highway Star • I Feel the Earth Move • Foreplay/Long Time (Long Time) • Point of Know Return • Sweet Home Alabama • Take the Long Way Home • Will It Go Round in Circles.
00700933 Keyboard Transcriptions $14.95

17. 1960s ROCK
Gimme Some Lovin' • Green Onions • I'm a Believer • Louie, Louie • Magic Carpet Ride • Oh, Pretty Woman • Runaway • The Twist.
00700935 Keyboard Transcriptions $14.99

18. 1950s ROCK
Blueberry Hill • Good Golly Miss Molly • Great Balls of Fire • The Great Pretender • Rock and Roll Is Here to Stay • Shake, Rattle and Roll • Tutti Frutti • What'd I Say.
00700934 Keyboard Transcriptions $14.95

19. JAZZ CLASSICS
Blues Etude • (They Long to Be) Close to You • Freeway • Lonely Woman • My Foolish Heart • Tin Tin Deo • Watch What Happens.
00701244 Keyboard Transcriptions $14.99

20. STEVIE WONDER
Boogie On Reggae Woman • Higher Ground • I Wish • Isn't She Lovely • Living for the City • Sir Duke • Superstition • You Are the Sunshine of My Life.
00701262 Keyboard Transcriptions $14.99

21. R&B
Baby Love • Easy • For Once in My Life • I Can't Help Myself (Sugar Pie, Honey Bunch) • I Heard It Through the Grapevine • Mess Around • Respect • Respect Yourself.
00701263 Keyboard Transcriptions $14.99

22. CAROLE KING
I Feel the Earth Move • It's Too Late • Jazzman • (You Make Me Feel Like) a Natural Woman • So Far Away • Sweet Seasons • Will You Love Me Tomorrow (Will You Still Love Me Tomorrow) • You've Got a Friend.
00701756 Keyboard Transcriptions $14.99

FOR MORE INFORMATION,
SEE YOUR LOCAL MUSIC DEALER,
OR WRITE TO:

HAL·LEONARD®
C O R P O R A T I O N
7777 W. BLUEMOUND RD. P.O. BOX 13819
MILWAUKEE, WISCONSIN 53213

Visit Hal Leonard Online at
www.halleonard.com

Prices, contents, and availability subject to change without notice.